Tamara Fonteyn

The Mandala Colouring Book

The Fractal Geometry of Beauty

TANOOK BOOKS

$$S = f_n(S)$$

$$x_{n+1} = ax_n + by_n + e$$
$$y_{n+1} = cx_n + dy_n + f$$

$$f_1(0.0x + 0.0y + 0.0, 0.0x + 0.16y + 0.0)$$
$$f_2(0.85x + 0.04y + 0.0; -0.04x + 0.85y + 1.6)$$
$$f_3(0.2x - 0.26y + 0.0; 0.23x + 0.22y + 1.6)$$
$$f_4(-0.15x + 0.28y + 0.0; 0.26x + 0.24y + 0.44)$$

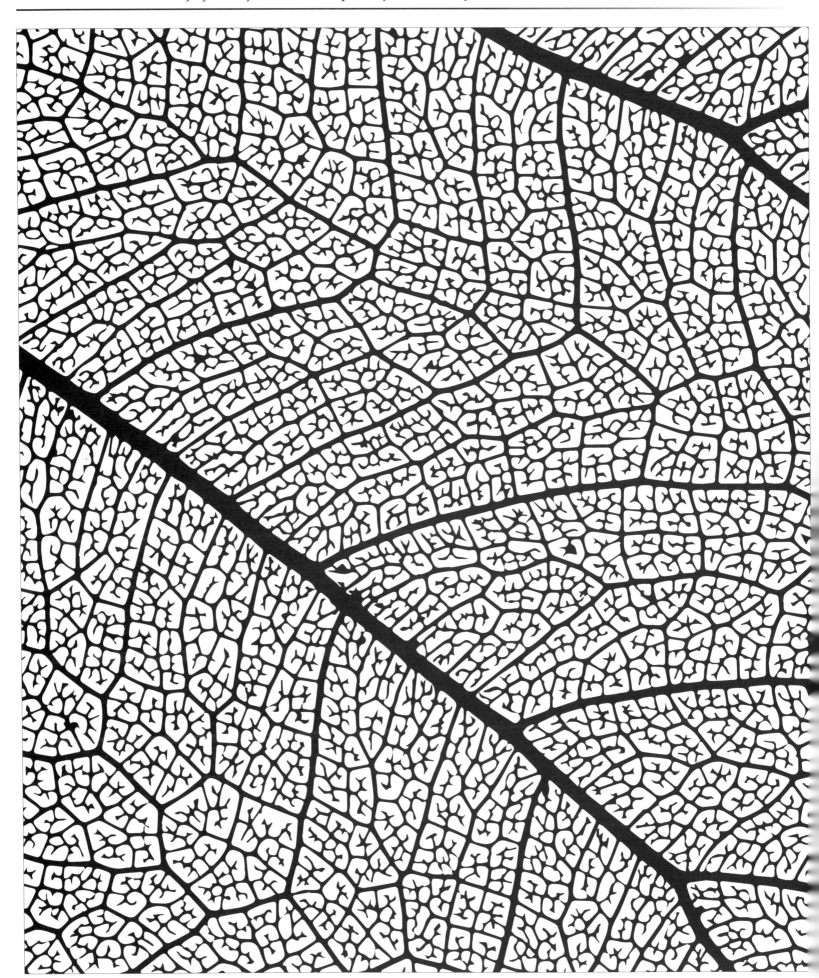

$$f(x) = x^7 - 1$$

$$x = x - (x^7 - 1) / 7z^6$$

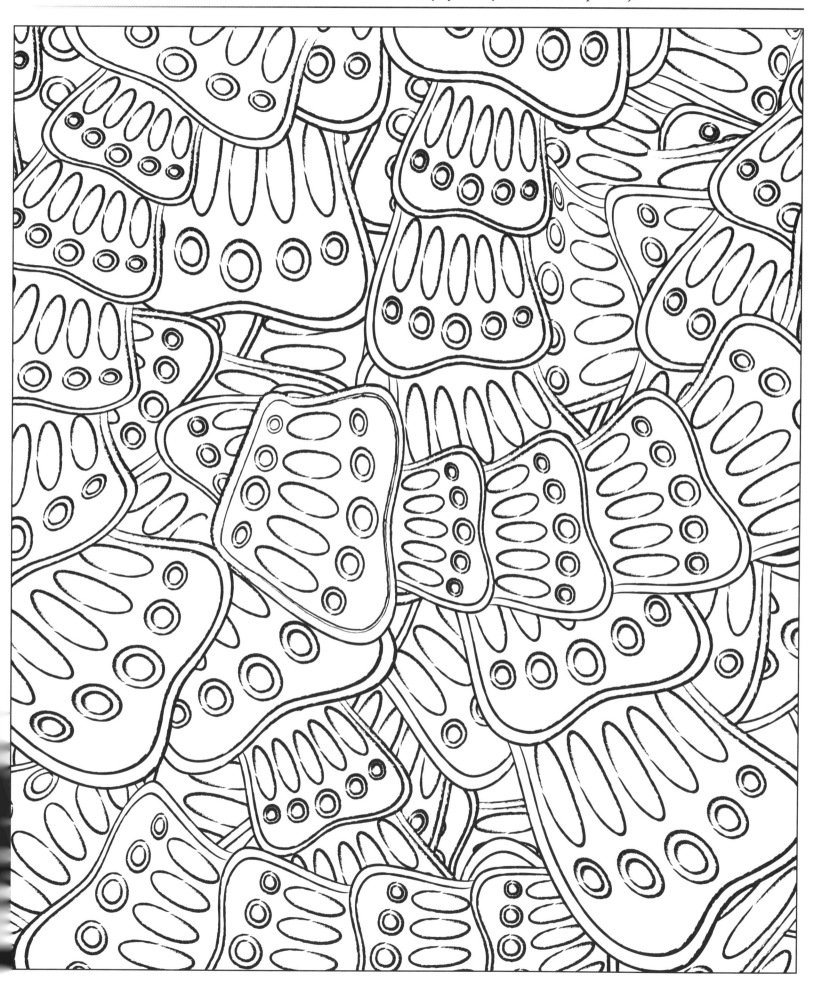

p = (3a)*(log 4/log 3)a

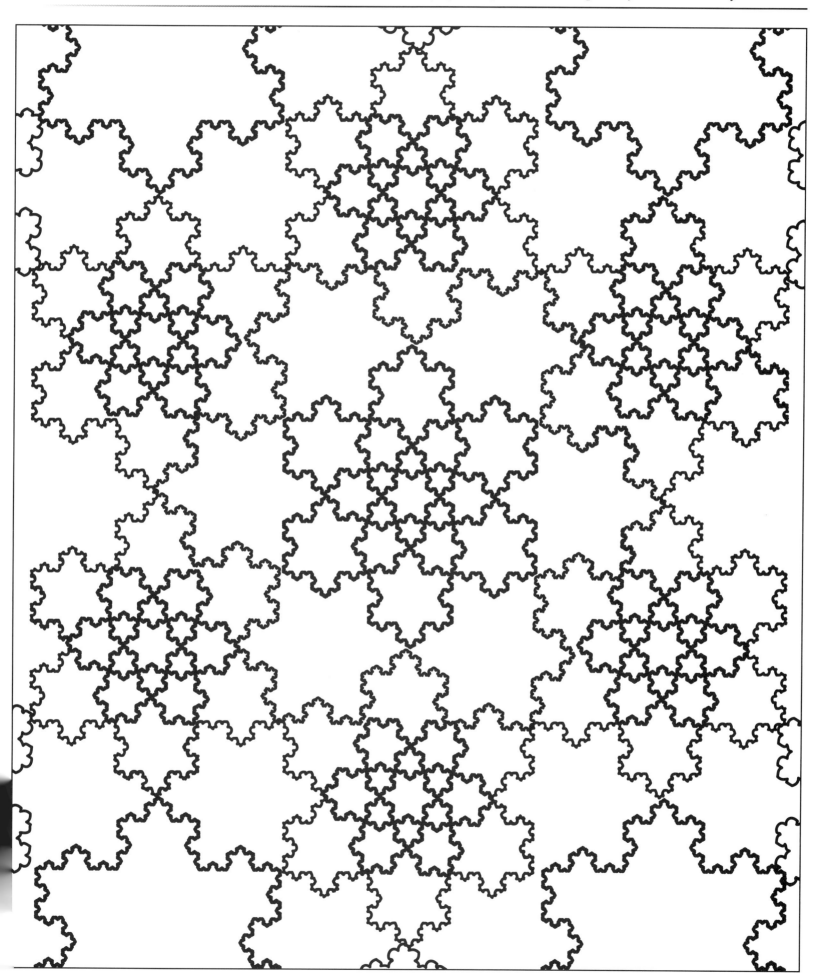

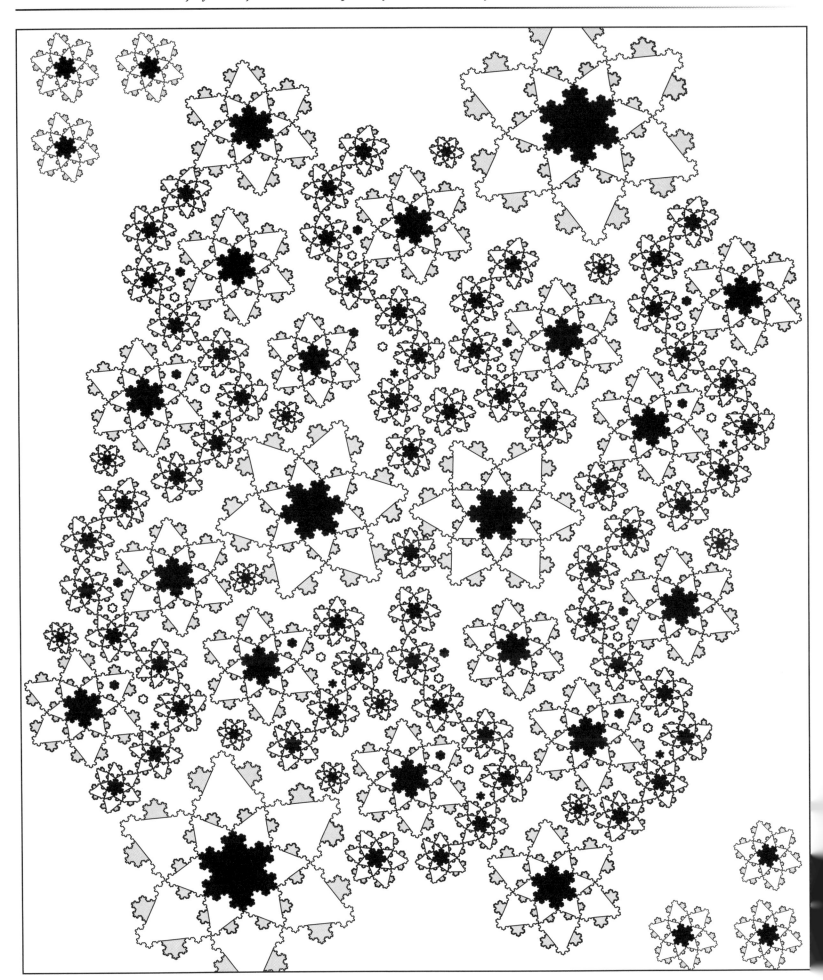

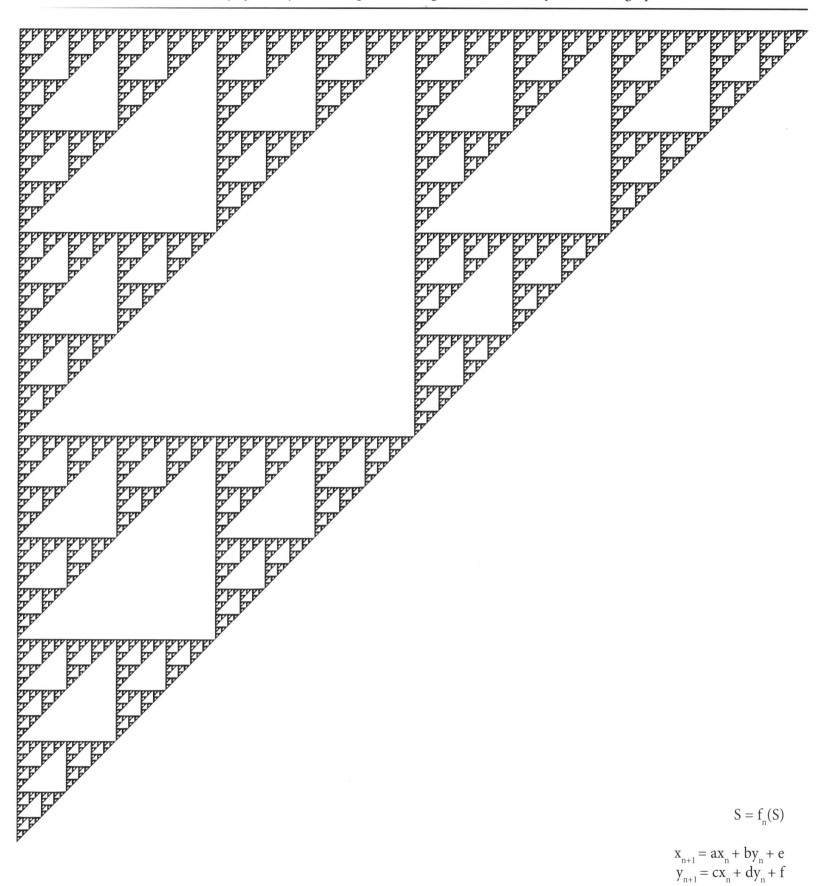

$$S = f_n(S)$$

$$x_{n+1} = ax_n + by_n + e$$
$$y_{n+1} = cx_n + dy_n + f$$

$$f_1(0.5x + 0.0y - 0.5; 0.0x + 0.5y + 0.5)$$
$$f_2(0.5x + 0.0y - 0.5; 0.0x + 0.5y - 0.5)$$
$$f_3(0.5x + 0.0y + 0.5; 0.0x + 0.5y - 0.5)$$

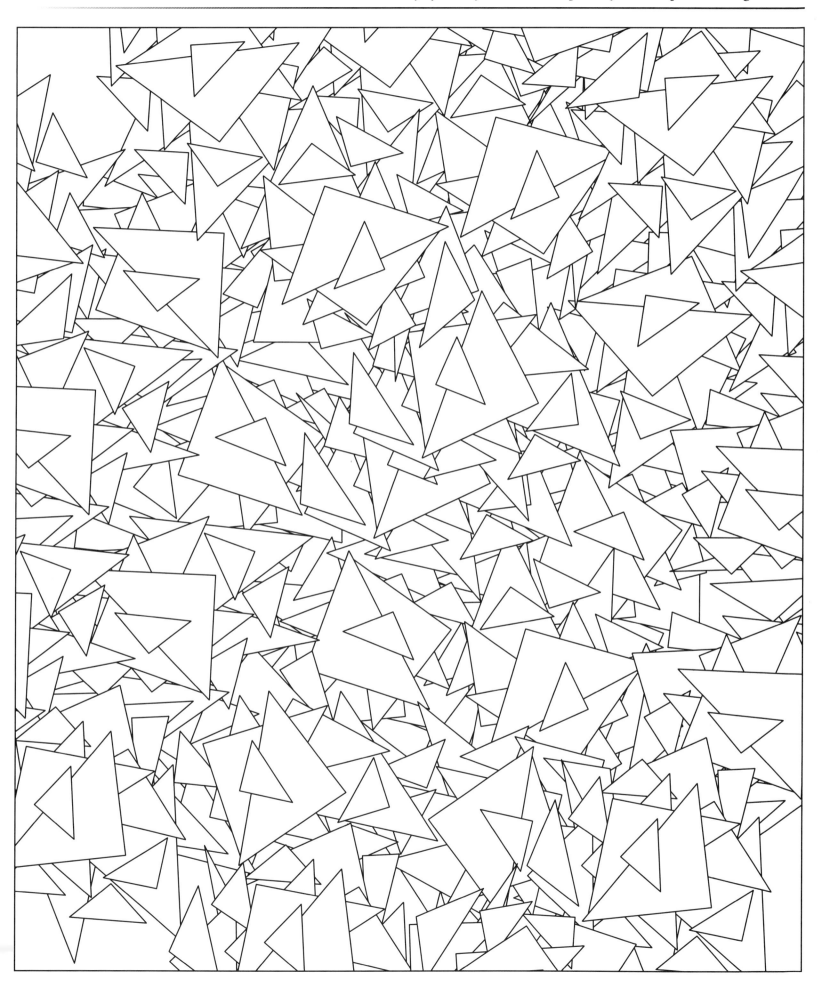

$$S = f_n(S)$$

$$x_{n+1} = ax_n + by_n + e$$
$$y_{n+1} = cx_n + dy_n + f$$

$$f_1(0.5x + 0.0y - 0.5; 0.0x + 0.5y + 0.5)$$
$$f_2(0.5x + 0.0y - 0.5; 0.0x + 0.5y - 0.5)$$
$$f_3(0.5x + 0.0y + 0.5; 0.0x + 0.5y - 0.5)$$

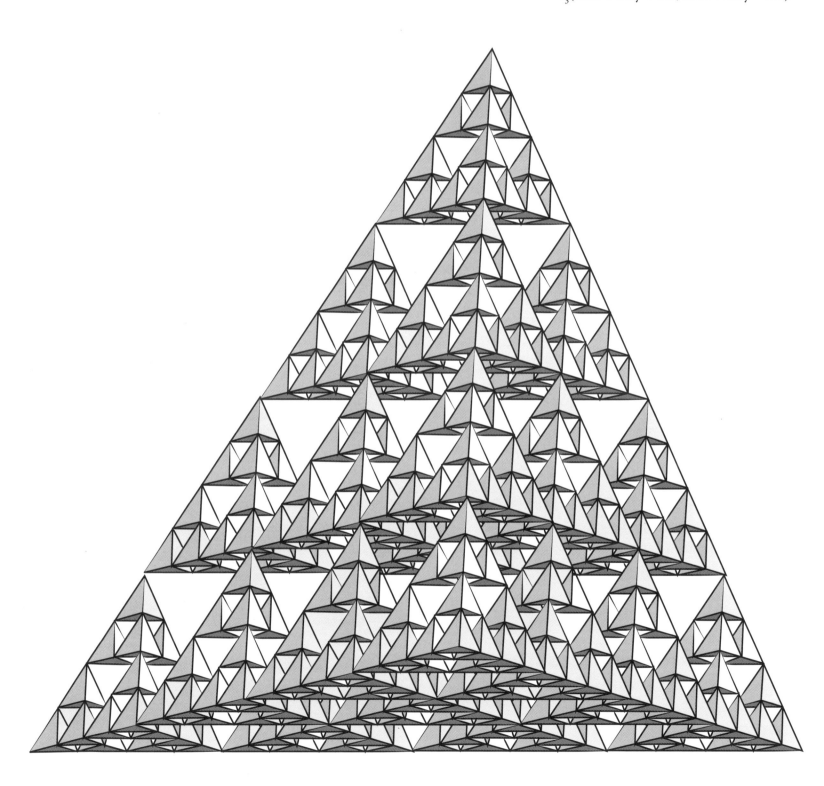

$$S_n = \left(\tfrac{8}{9}\right)^n, \; n = 0, 1, 2\ldots$$

$$S_{n+1} = \tfrac{8}{9} S_n, \; n = 0, 1, 2\ldots; \; S_0 = 1$$

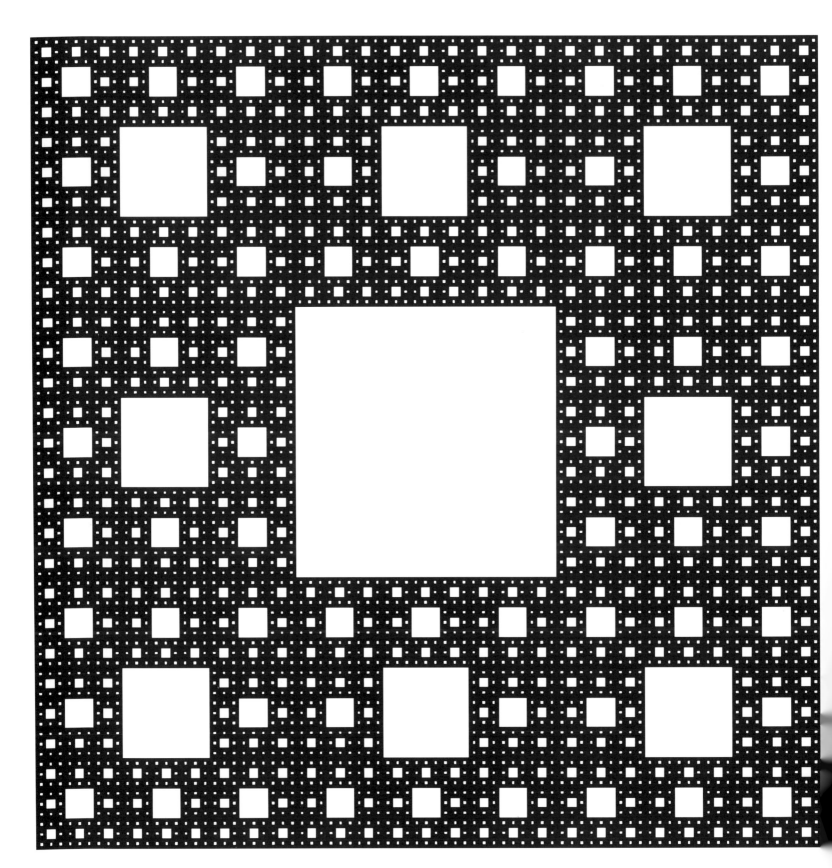

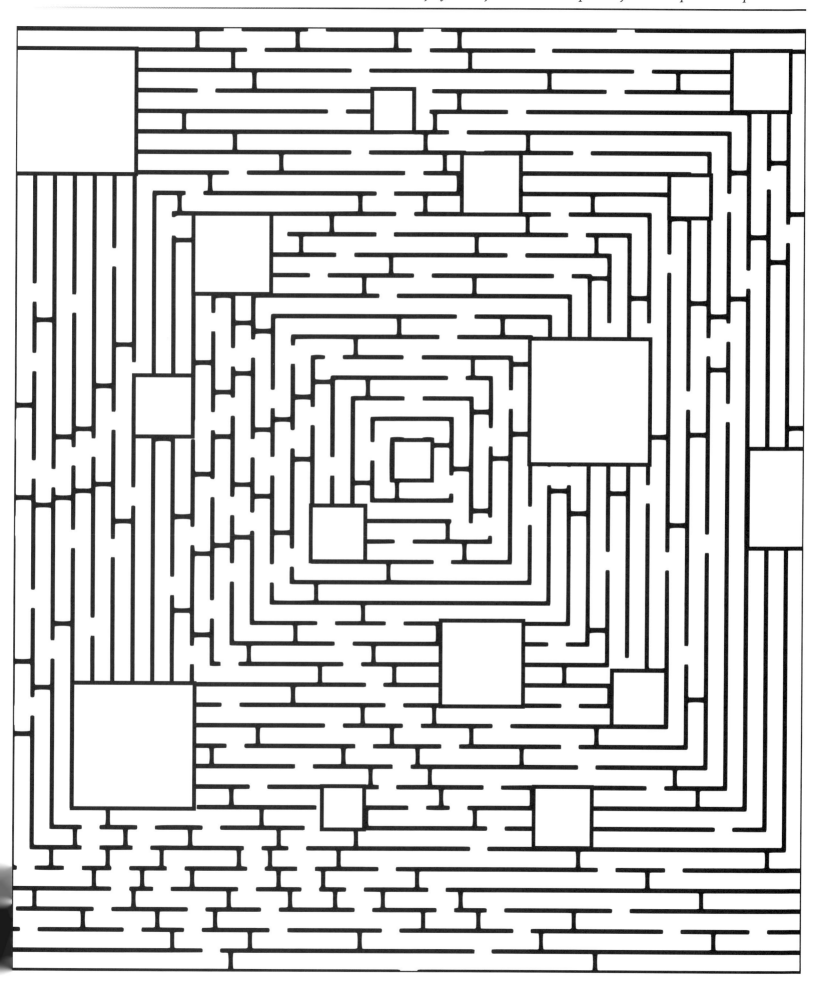

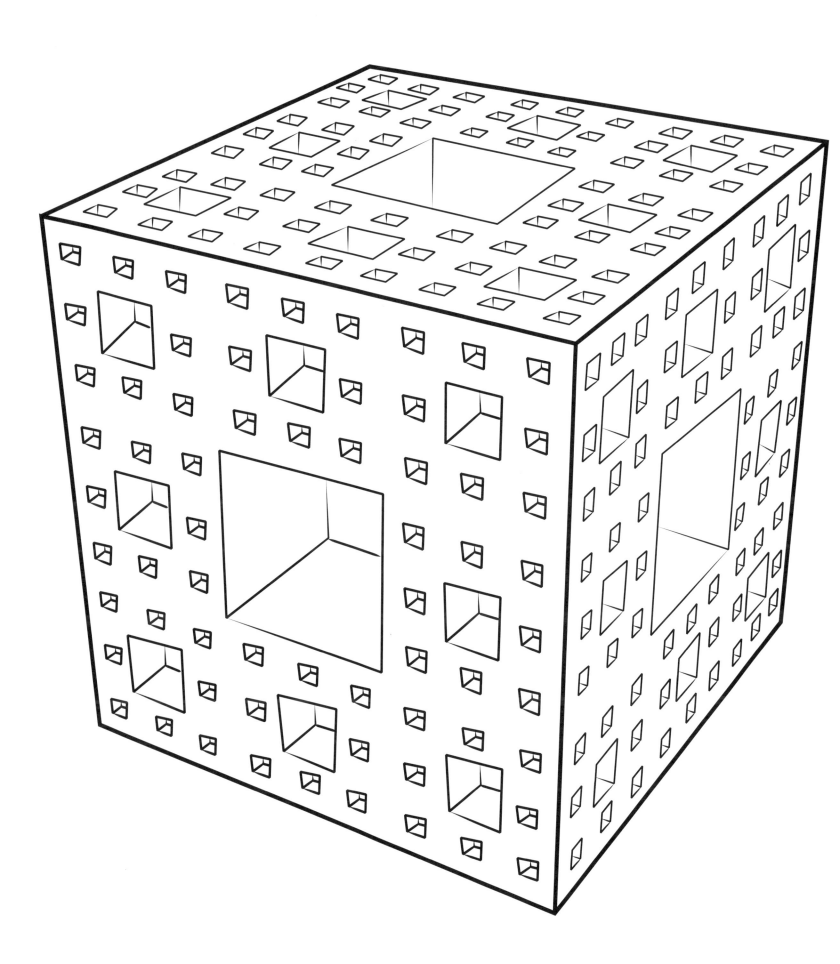

$$a2 + b2 + c2 + d2 = 2ab + 2ac + 2ad + 2bc + 2bd + 2cd$$
$$(-n, n + 1, n(n + 1), n(n + 1) + 1)$$

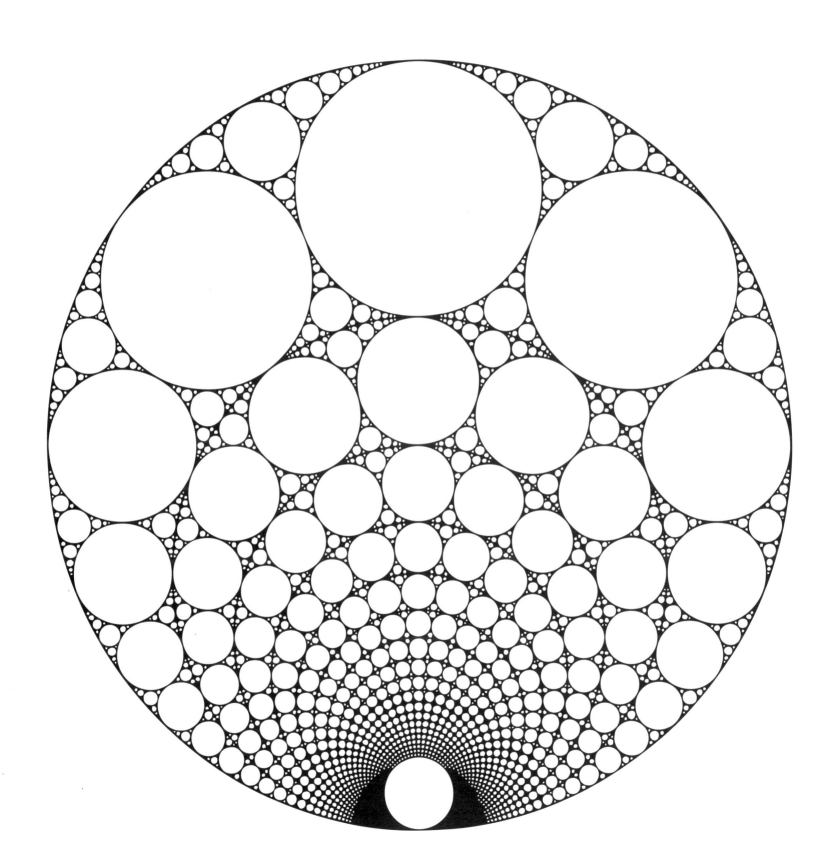

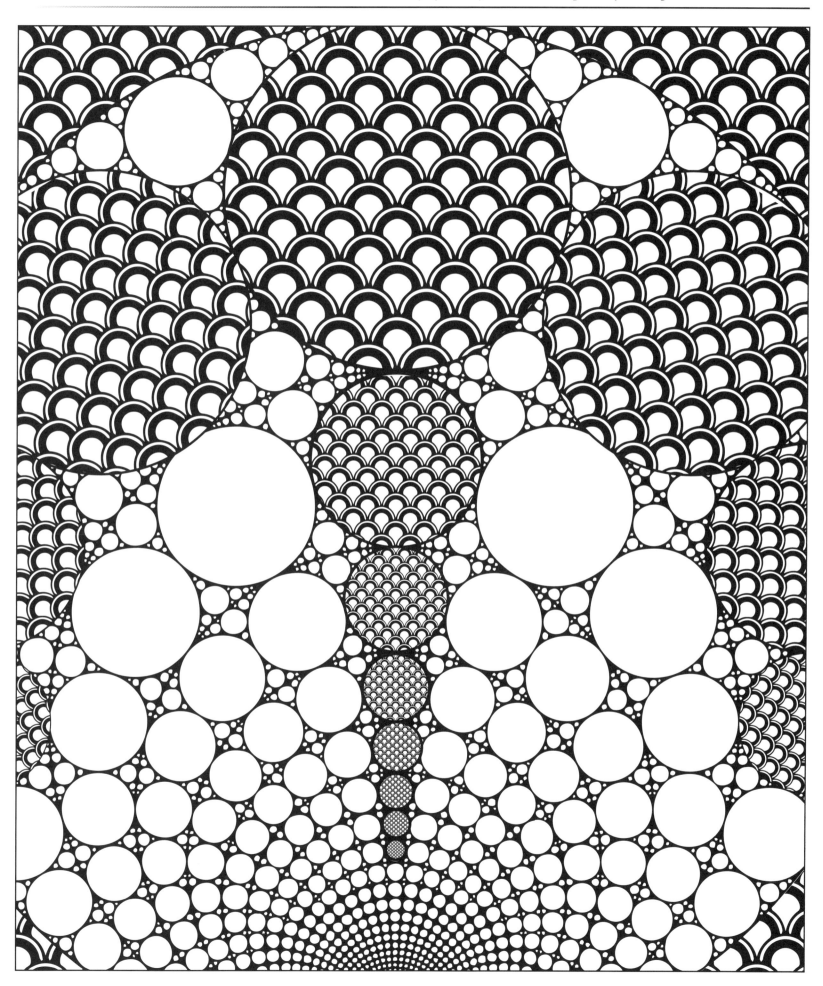

$$S = f_n(S)$$

$$x_{n+1} = ax_n + by_n + e$$
$$y_{n+1} = cx_n + dy_n + f$$

$f_1(0.787879x - 0.424242y + 1.758647; 0.242424x + 0.859848y + 1.408065)$
$f_2(-0.121212x + 0.257576y - 6.721654; 0.151515x + 0.053030y + 1.377236)$
$f_3(0.181818x - 0.136364y + 6.086107; 0.090909x + 0.181818y + 1.568035)$

$$S = f_n(S)$$

$$x_{n+1} = ax_n + by_n + e$$
$$y_{n+1} = cx_n + dy_n + f$$

$$f_1(0.14x + 0.01y - 1.31; \; 0.0x + 0.51y + 0.1)$$
$$f_2(0.43x + 0.52y + 1.49; \; -0.45x + 0.5y - 0.75)$$
$$f_3(0.45x - 0.49y - 1.62; \; 0.47x + 0.47y - 0.74)$$
$$f_4(0.49x + 0.0y + 0.02; \; 0.0x + 0.51y + 1.62)$$

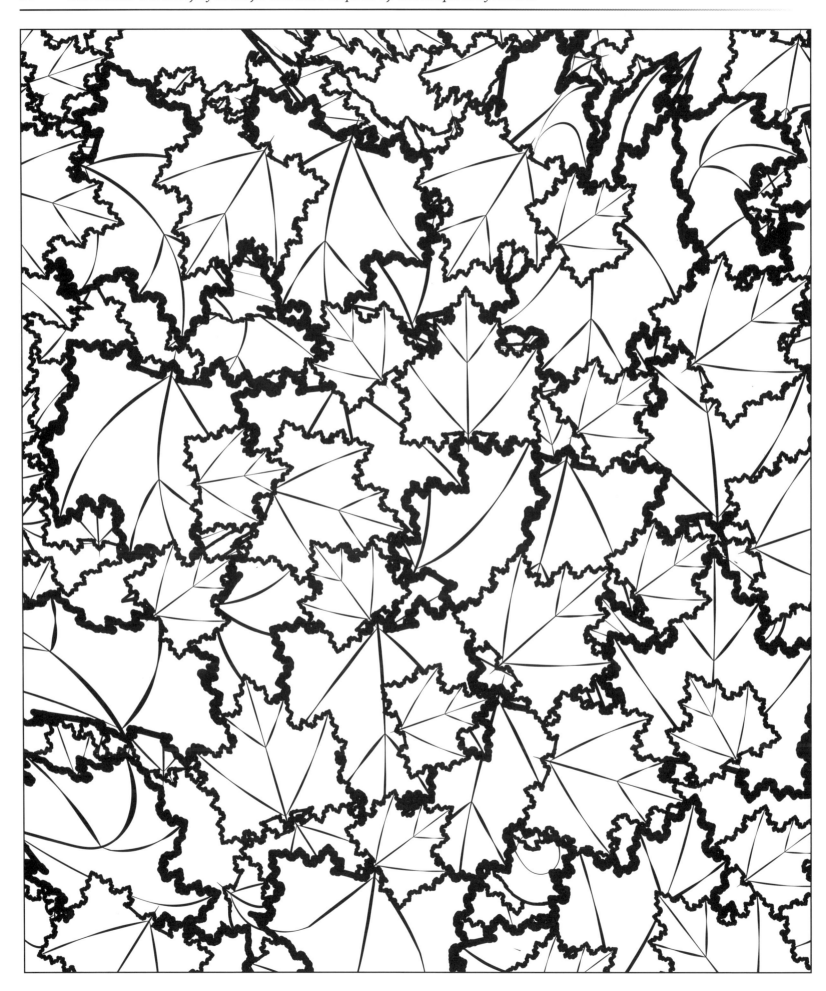

$$f(x) = x^5 - 1$$

$$x = x - (x^5 - 1) / 5z^4$$

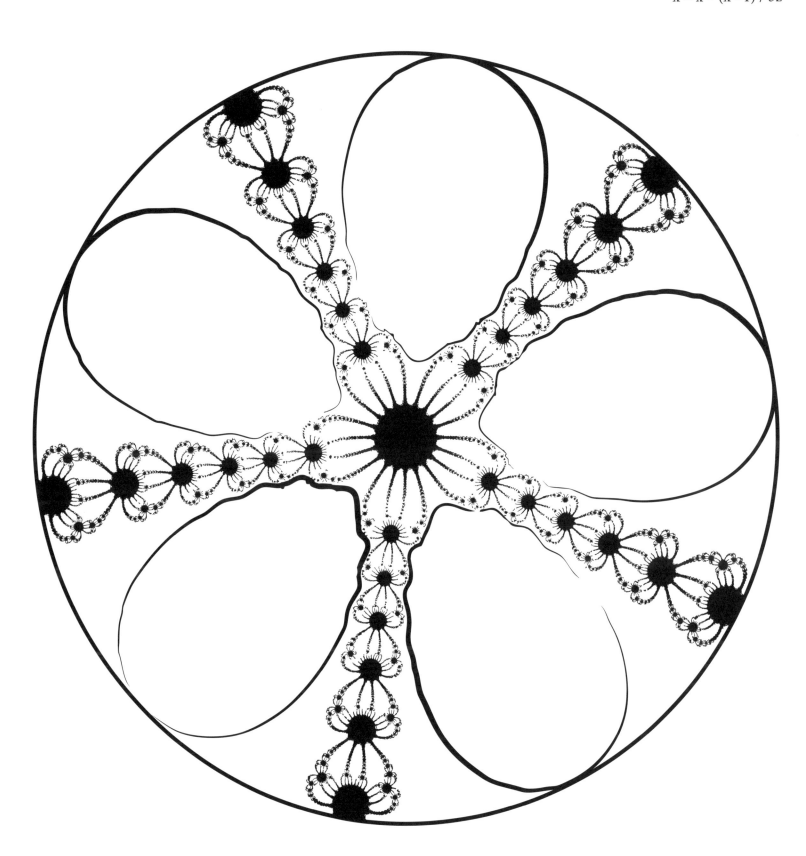

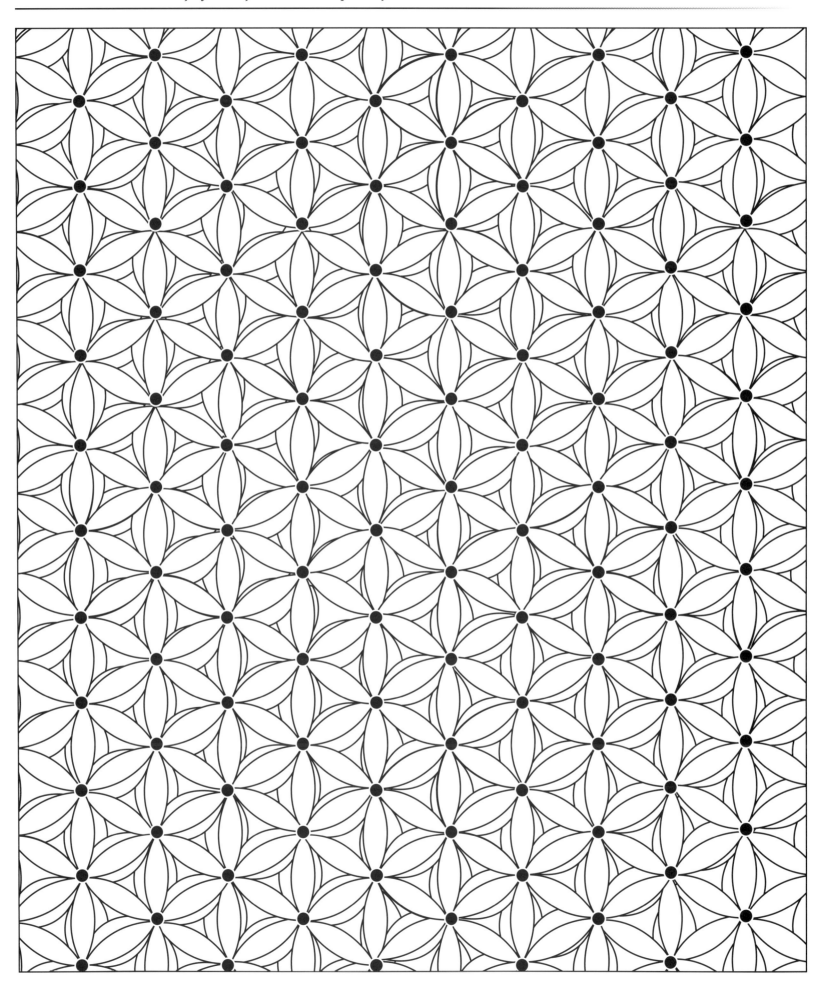

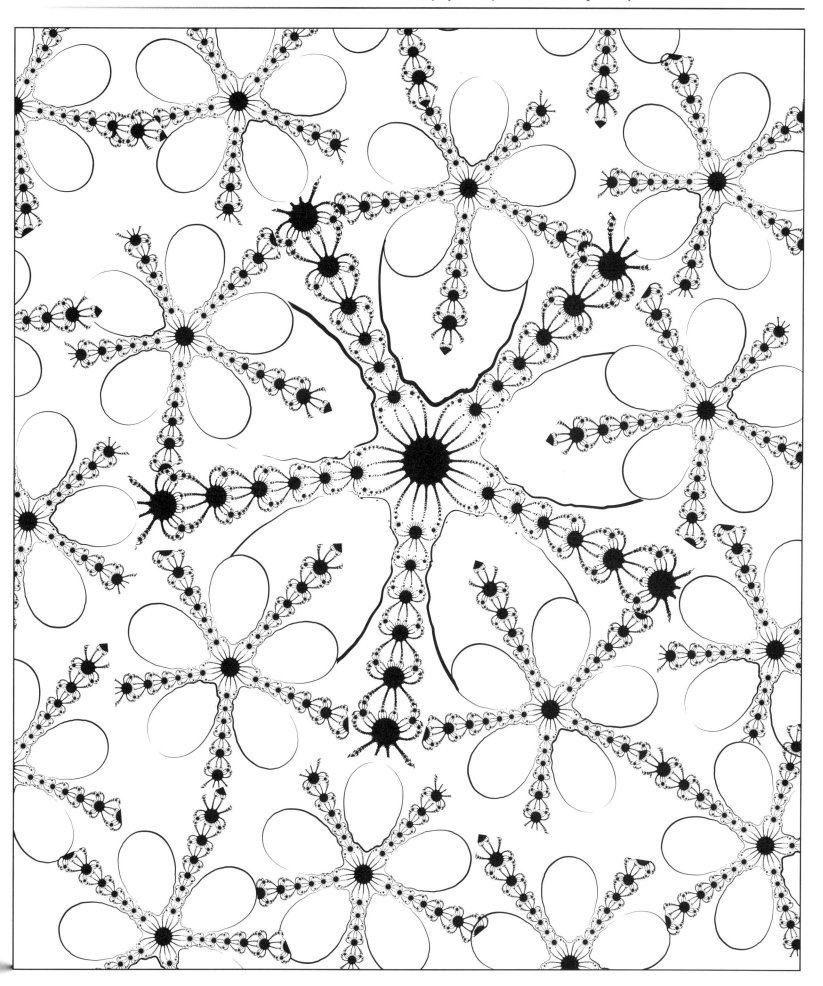

$$z \leftarrow z2 + c$$

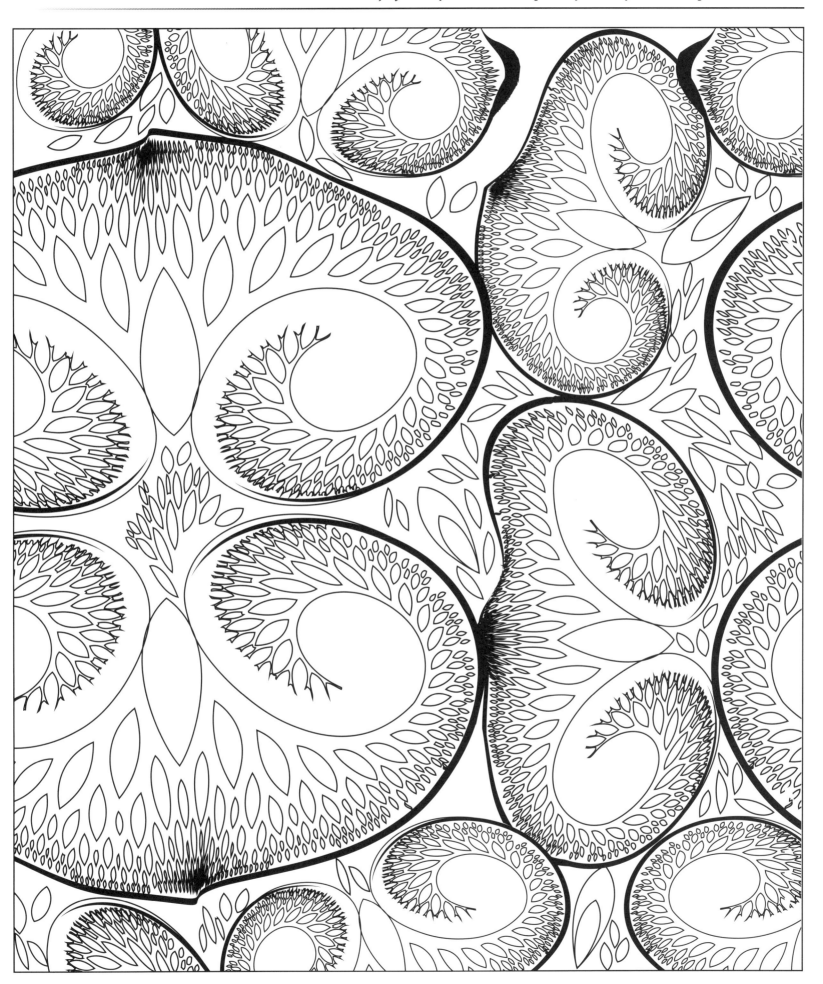

$$f(x) = x^4 - 1$$

$$x = x - (x^4 - 1) / 4z^3$$

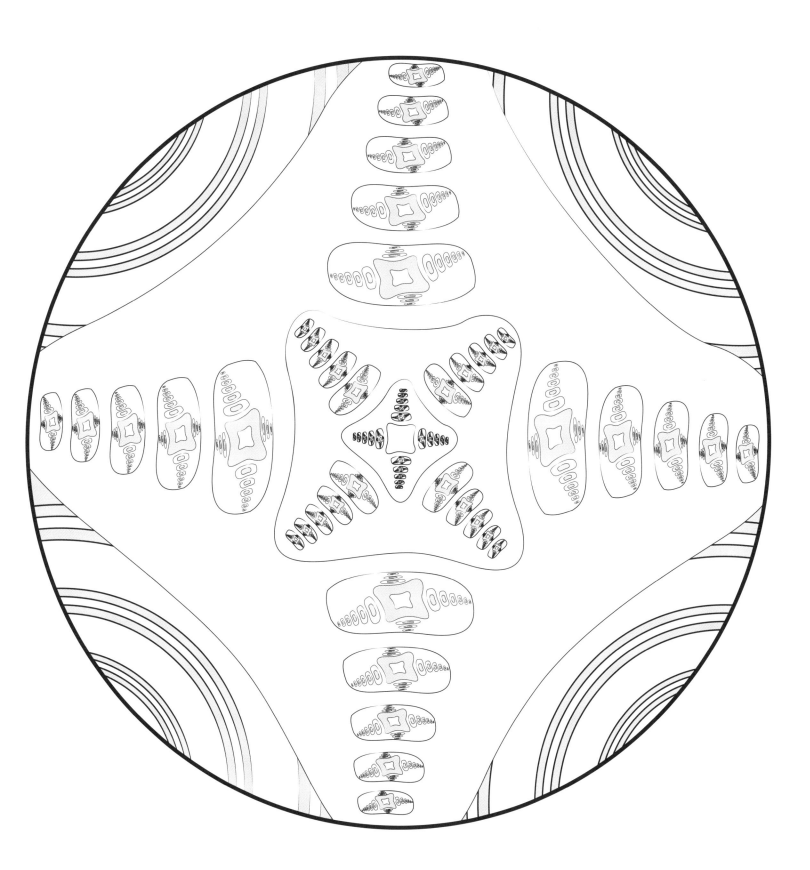

$$S = f_n(S)$$

$$x_{n+1} = ax_n + by_n + e$$
$$y_{n+1} = cx_n + dy_n + f$$

$$f_1(0.05x + 0.0y - 0.06;\ 0.0x + 0.4y - 0.47)$$
$$f_2(-0.05x + 0.0y - 0.06;\ 0.0x - 0.4y - 0.47)$$
$$f_3(0.03x - 0.14y - 0.16;\ 0.0x + 0.26y - 0.01)$$
$$f_4(-0.03x + 0.14y - 0.16;\ 0.0x - 0.26y - 0.01)$$
$$f_5(0.56x + 0.44y + 0.3;\ -0.37x + 0.51y + 0.15)$$
$$f_6(0.19x + 0.07y - 0.2;\ -0.1x + 0.15y + 0.28)$$
$$f_7(-0.33x - 0.34y - 0.54;\ -0.33x + 0.34y + 0.39)$$

$$\text{blanc}\,(x) = \sum_{n=0}^{\infty} \frac{s(2^n x)}{2^n}$$